The Barnyard Bunch

SILLY SHEE

Ryan James

NorwoodHouse Press

Cataloging-in-Publication Data

Names: James, Ryan.
Title: Silly sheep / Ryan James.
Description: Buffalo, NY : Norwood House Press, 2026. | Series: The barnyard bunch | Includes glossary and index.
Identifiers: ISBN 9781978574380 (pbk.) | ISBN 9781978574397 (library bound) | ISBN 9781978574403 (ebook)
Subjects: LCSH: Sheep--Juvenile literature. | Livestock--Juvenile literature.
Classification: LCC SF375.2 J359 2026 | DDC 636.3--dc23

Published in 2026 by
Norwood House Press
2544 Clinton Street
Buffalo, NY 14224

Designer: Rhea Magaro
Editor: Kim Thompson

Photo credits: Cover, p. 1 Eric Gevaert/Shutterstock.com; p. 5 Heath Johnson/Shutterstock.com; p. 6 New Africa/Shutterstock.com; p. 7 miroslavmisiura/Shutterstock.com; p. 8 Josh Namdar/Shutterstock.com; p. 9 Juice Verve/Shutterstock.com; p. 10 Clara Bastian/Shutterstock.com; p. 11 aodaodaodaod/Shutterstock.com; pp. 12,1 3 Kuttelvaserova Stuchelova/Shutterstock.com; p. 14 Dagmar Hijmans/Shutterstock.com; p. 15 nadtochiy/Shutterstock.com; p. 17 dibrova/Shutterstock.com; pp. 18, 19 Janice Chen/Shutterstock.com; p. 21 Allexxandar/Shutterstock.com;

Printed in the United States of America

CPSIA compliance information: Batch #CSNHP26: For further information contact Norwood House Press at 1-800-237-9932.

TABLE OF CONTENTS

SILLY SHEEP

Sheep are farm animals.

They live in the barnyard.

People who take care of sheep are called shepherds.

Some farms have dogs to **herd** sheep. Sheepdogs and other dogs protect sheep from **predators**.

HOW SHEEP LOOK

Sheep have heavy **wool** coats.

Their wool comes in many colors.

Farmers **shear** sheep to get their wool. Wool is used to make clothes and fabrics.

Sheep have short tails and ears.

Sheep have four legs with **hooves**.

HOW SHEEP SOUND

Sheep make noises that sound like "baa." This is called **bleating**.

Sheep bleat to **communicate** with each other.

WHAT SHEEP EAT

Sheep are **herbivores**. They eat only plants.

When they are outside, sheep eat grass. When they are inside, sheep eat **hay**.

Sheep like to **graze** in **pastures**. Some sheep travel from pasture to pasture to find healthy grass to eat.

HOW SHEEP GROW UP

Baby sheep are called lambs. Lambs bleat to their mothers.

Lambs are very active. They like to play.

FUN ON THE FARM

A group of sheep is called a flock.

Flocks of sheep run around together.

GLOSSARY

bleating (BLEE-ting): making a cry that sounds like "baa"

communicate (kuh-MYOO-ni-kate): to share information and feelings

graze (graze): to feed on grass that is growing in a field

hay (hay): long grass that is cut, dried, and used as food for farm animals

herbivores (HUR-buh-vorz): animals that eat only plants

herd (hurd): to gather sheep together and move them as a group

hooves (hoovz): hard parts that cover the feet of sheep, horses, and other animals

pastures (PAS-churz): grassy fields where animals graze

predators (PRED-uh-turz): wolves and other animals that hunt animals for food

shear (sheer): to cut the wool off sheep

wool (wul): the soft, thick, curly hair of sheep that can be spun into yarn and used to make cloth

THINKING QUESTIONS

1. What are baby sheep called?
2. Name three body parts that sheep have.
3. How are sheep protected on farms?
4. How do sheep communicate?
5. What is a group of sheep called?

INDEX

ABOUT THE AUTHOR

Ryan James lives in the mountains of North Carolina, where he goes hiking with his dog Bailey. He loves fly fishing, visiting farms in the area, and picking fresh produce. He has always enjoyed writing and wrote his first book as a teenager.